WALKING BETWEEN
THE SHADOWS

WALKING
BETWEEN
THE SHADOWS

NOAH JAMES

iUniverse, Inc.
New York   Bloomington

Walking between the shadows

iUniverse books may be ordered through booksellers or by contacting:

iUniverse
1663 Liberty Drive
Bloomington, IN 47403
www.iuniverse.com
1-800-Authors (1-800-288-4677)

Because of the dynamic nature of the Internet, any Web addresses or links contained in this book may have changed since publication and may no longer be valid. The views expressed in this work are solely those of the author and do not necessarily reflect the views of the publisher, and the publisher hereby disclaims any responsibility for them.

ISBN: 978-1-4502-2618-9 (sc)
ISBN: 978-1-4502-2619-6 (ebk)

Printed in the United States of America

iUniverse rev. date: 05/27/2010

This book is dedicated to my mother May Wiertalla, my daughter Tiffanie Arnold to whom I love very much and in loving memory of Deanna Prout

A special dedication for my friends Faith Janick and Hope Janick, thanks for showing me the light every chance you got and to Ibite Back, I love you all very much.

After All

I will give you
A diamond ring
And all those other
Pretty things
A great big house
I will buy for you
And fill it with
Everything that's new
A looking glass
That will not break
And I'll draw a bath
For you to take
I'll buy you a dress
For the ball
Why do I do this
Cause I love you after all

Am I not sane

I want to go home
But am I that strong
With one slice of my wrist
I don't know what went wrong
My mom and dad
All they did was cry
I don't really know
If I want to get by
To be best of the best
Now don't let go of the reins
So tell me now
Am I not sane
It was all their fault
They need to bleed
How can they be better
I'll bring them to their knees
I'll show them who the best is
Then they will see
No one can ever
Be better than me
To be best of the best
Now don't let go of the reins
So tell me now
Am I not sane

ANGEL SENT

God sent you an angel
From heaven above
God sent you an angel
To show his true love
He gave me a halo
Shining so bright
To teach you to see
All through the night
He gave me these wings
But not for me
To teach you to fly
So you can be free
He gave me this harp
With songs like a dove
To teach you to sing
And learn how to love
You say you are not learning
Well do not dread
Because you are the teacher
And I'm learning instead

This poem was written
For my best friend
Karen Eggleston

ASK HIM

If you are going down your path
And come to a fork in the road
Looking at both
And don't know which way to go
Sit down and look up high
Fold your hands and say a hymn
You seek the way
Ask him
You walk in darkness
And don't know why
All you want to do
Is sit down and cry
Get down on your knees
Fold your hands and say a hymn
You seek the light
Ask him
You look inside
And your soul is stained
For causing so many
So much pain
Fall on the ground and close your eyes
Cover your head and cry a hymn
You seek to be saved
Ask him

Before

Things they change
Everywhere you look
In just a moment
That's all it took
Winter becomes spring
New becomes old
Nothing stays the same
Or so I'm told
People are no different
As I can plainly see
Good become bad
Then they belong to me
I am not immune to
The changes that are made
I do not regret the things I did
Or the price that I paid
I think I belong here
The place I have gone
You will be here too
And it won't be long
I'm loved by all here
Who walk the eternal night
Before I was king of darkness
I too walked the light

BEST OF FRIENDS

You touched my heart
When you touched my hand
Forever behind you
I will stand
Through thick and thin
We will always be
The best of friends
You and me

This poem was written for
Ankii Andel my good friend

DARK PRINCE

Darkness falls across the land
Giving me the upper hand
Awaken from my slumber sleep
To walk through the darkness deep
To catch the mortals is my plan
And drink the blood from every man
I see in your eyes all your tears
Each time as I draw near
Scared I see and it makes since
For I am the Dark Prince

BLEED MY LOVE

Come with me
Let's go for a walk
No need for tears
No need to talk
I see all those demons
That hide inside you
I've seen them before
This is nothing new
There is no other way
That I can think of
With all my heart
Bleed my love
Now not to worry
You'll be alright
I will show you
No need to fight
I'm going to get them out
Then you will see
You won't be like the others
You will thank me
There is no other way
That I can think of
With all my heart
Bleed my love
They shine so bright
All those pretty lights
That's what they said
The voices in my head
There is no other way
That I can think of
With all my heart
Bleed my love

Bottom of my bottle

I still remember the fight we had
That tore us apart
All the things that was said
Must have broken your heart
I still remember the look in your eyes
When you ran out the door
I never really knew then
That it was you that I was looking for
How could I have let you walk away
I knew I should have followed
Now I'm just looking for you
At the bottom of my bottle
So this is the price
For looking the other way
I wish I knew what to say to you
That would make you want to stay
I should have said I love you
And I thought that you should know
I should have said baby please come back
Baby please don't go
How could I let you walk out that door
I knew I should have followed
Now I'm just looking for you
At the bottom of my bottle
You walk in the door
And you walk right up to me
I wrap my arms around you
But it's just a memory
How could I let you walk out the door
I knew I should have followed
Now I'm just looking for you
At the bottom of my bottle

By your side

I look for him
Everywhere I go
He is all around us
This I know
He is the light
He is the way
He is love
No matter what they say
What if I find him
What's in store
Will he look at me
And wish I were more
Will he know me
Will he recognize my face
Why does he hide
Not even a trace
I lift my head
And search the sky
I scream and shout
I yell and cry
What did I do
Why do you hide
He whispers I don't
I've been by your side

CALLING YOU

You hear me whisper
In the dark
You feel my touch
Cause a spark
You start to walk now
In slumber sleep
No one can stop me
You're mine to keep
Someone see us
They start to yell
All you hear is
The sounds of bells
It's midnight now
You're at my door
Soon you'll be
Alive no more
Open your eyes
It's time you knew
That it was Dracula
That was calling you

Can you hear me

Hello it's been awhile since we talked
I hope you remember me
I ran into some trouble here
And I don't know if you can see
I really don't want to be a bother
And I know it's nothing new
I don't know if you can do anything
But I was told to talk to you
They say you won't judge
Or look down on me
I don't know if I'm doing this right
Can you hear me
I really try to do good
I don't know how my life fell apart
I don't know if I have the right
They said just talk from the heart
I know you sent your son to us
And he died for all our sins
You're probably wondering where I've been
I really don't know where to begin
I guess I lost my faith
When things started to wrong
I guess you see by now
That I'm not really that strong
Well I guess I should go now
This is just how it's going to be
I've taken up enough of your time I think
Can you hear me

CLUBBIN

You get out of the shower
And search for clothes
For what kind
You don't know
Open the door
And step outside
As you see the people
Walk on by
You take a breath
And start to move
You hear something
And start to groove
Hearing the music
From the street
You open the door
And feel the beat
To the dance floor
You must go
As you feel the music
Start to flow
You feel something
Inside start rubbin
Not to worry
Now you're clubbin

COLLECTOR OF BONES

In the shadows is where I stay
Watching you as you walk along
You are my sweet, sweet prey
And I'll catch you before long
I hear your breathe quicken
As your heart starts to beat
I can sense your fear
By the quickening of your feet
What I am time has forgot
Where I come from was never known
I'm the one you heard of but never seen
For I am the collector of bones
I kill without mercy
But never a stone out of place
Just one single bone
And the horror on their face
There is never a trace
That tells that I was near
They must have just died
And the bone just disappeared
What I am time has forgot
Where I come from was never known
I'm the one you heard of but never seen
For I am the collector of bones
Now that I am here
This is the end
You have stumbled into
A place you shouldn't have been
With a flick of my knife
Your blood starts to spill
I lean in to hear your last breathe
And then you go still
What I am time has forgot
Where I come from was never known
I'm the one you heard of but never seen
For I am the collector of bones

DAMNED

Hush my darling
Don't you cry
Sit right there
I'll tell you why
Life was fun
You had a ball
You told your tale
You lived it all
You made your mark
You made your score
You made men suffer
Their hearts you tore
You made them pay
You took your toll
You ripped them apart
You sold their souls
No don't try to lie
Or try to scam
Cause now my darling
Your soul is damned

DARK PRINCE

Darkness falls across the land
Giving me the upper hand
Awaken from my slumber sleep
To walk through the darkness deep
To catch the mortals is my plan
And drink the blood from every man
I see in your eyes all your tears
Each time as I draw near
Scared I see and it makes since
For I am the Dark Prince

DARKNESS IS COMING

Darkness is coming
It's coming for me
I have nowhere to hide
None that I see
I have to run
Run from this place
But I know that the darkness
Is my fate
Darkness is coming
From where I know not
Time is the only
Thing I forgot
I look in my soul
And there I can see
The darkness that is coming
Is inside of me

DEALER OF PAIN

Sit right down
Let me deal you in
No need to ante
Let's just begin
The game is
Best out of five
If I win I get
To take what's mine
What will be mine
Will be your soul
If you win
You get this stack of gold
I see you like that
Oh what a grin
Well sign right there
Oh sorry I win
Now just sit down
Try to restrain
Just so you know
I'm the dealer of pain

DEATH

Ah death how I long for the day
When you come for me at last
To wrap me in your sweet embrace
And take me to my eternal resting place
Ah death I feel your sweet embrace
You chill me to the bone
You show me peace at last
As I take my dying breathe

DEATH IS COMING

I lie here in bed
Looking out at the sky
They say I'll be ok
But I know that's a lie
Mom and dad are here
I cannot make out what they say
Grandma and grandpa are here too
But they already passed away
There'll be no prom for me
I really wanted to go
They want me to go with them
I look at mom, I really don't know
Is she going to be alright
She won't have her boys
What about Tommy
No one will be there to hide his toys
I look at Grandma and she smiles
I know it has to be
Death is coming
It's coming for me

DO YOU KNOW ME

I do not belong here
This is not my place
I do not recognize
Anyone's face
This has to be a mistake
This has to be a dream
I want to know
Do you know me
Why can't I move
You have to let me go
They're going to kill me
What do you mean no
This has to be a mistake
I just want to scream
I want to know
Do you know me
Okay that's it
You think you've won
Kill me and they will hunt you
It has probably begun
This has been your mistake
Go ahead assonate me
I want to know
Do you know me

DRIVEN BY MY MADNESS

You sit there and judge me
I know that you do
You are all out to get me
I know this is true
You say that it is ok
Everything is fine
It will all work out
It's just a matter of time
I read the message in your eyes
Your tale has just been told
This charade has gone on long enough
It is really getting quite old
Your treachery has gone on long enough
It is time you should pay
I should get you before you get me
At least that's what the voices say
What have I done, no I am king
What did I do to you
I ruled this kingdom with honesty
And valor that was true
Now I see you want the throne
I see it in your eyes
That's why you stood here today
Telling those filthy lies
I see you brought your men in white
And I don't buy all this sadness
Don't you dare try to say that
I'm driven by my madness

ENJOY

Go ahead and smile
While you look back at me
Go ahead and laugh
At the tears that you see
Go ahead and yell
Those words that you say
Go ahead and do all those things
That hurt me that way
Enjoy the work
That you have done
I should just
Turn around and run
Enjoy the way
You make me hide
Enjoy the way
You tare me up inside
In the shadows I'll go
So you can't see
It is so hard to hide
When you are me

FALL FROM GRACE

I keep on searching
Trying to find my way
Everywhere I turn
It all looks the same
I hear a voice
I fall to my knees
I look toward the sky
As I start to plea
I fall to the ground
As I see the light
I close my eyes
It's shines so bright
I feel the heat
It does not burn
It touches my soul
It starts to yearn
I hear his voice
You're in the right place
Just look for me
When you fall from grace

FIND ME

I'm looking for a place
Where people are kind
Where people do not hate
And love is not blind
Where the color of skin
Does not make a man
Where everyone gives
A helping hand
Where people are judge
For who they are
Where people are free to love
Who holds their heart
If you find the place
Where people are free
Then you come
And find me

FREDDIE

You know Freddie
Is his name
Killing you in your sleep
Is his game
He sleeps while
You are awake
And in your sleep
Your soul he'll take
The souls of the children
Keep him strong
And for him
Nothing can go wrong
He is getting close
And it's your funeral
Cause Freddie Kruger
He is eternal

FROM HIS EYES

Life is not fair from where you're at
Under that cap or pretty bows
From a scrape from falling of your bike
Or the tears when you stubbed your toe
You looking up as they say no
You feel you're on trial
That's not fair you kick and scream
You know I'm no child
I'm grown now I'm almost three
And I don't need a potty chair
In three more years I'll be four
And I won't need a booster chair
When do I get to stay up all night
And do what big people do
Sit there on the couch drinking hot chocolate
While yelling at the news
There is something you should know
And I don't want you to get riled
Even when you go off to school
From his eyes you'll always be his child

GATES OF HELL

There is one thing
I would like to say
My love for you
Grows everyday
From the first day
That I saw you
From that moment
I knew
That with you no other
Can rise above
My heart flutters
On the wings of a dove
To show you
My words are true
There is one thing
I would gladly do
With the stroke of midnight
With the toll of the bells
I would gladly stand
At the gates of Hell

GIVE NOT TAKE

A man who gives
But does not take
Has the world for his own
A man who takes
But does not give
Lives all alone
For what I am saying
Is quite clear
You give love
Not take my dear

Happy Halloween

It is our hour, ghost and goblins
It is time to come out
Witches, vampires, and werewolves too
To scare and haunt is what we are about
Don't try to run and hide
It won't do you any good
We are all around you
Up and down the neighborhood
We know you very well
So don't try to say you forgot
Just give us what we want
And trick you we will not
You don't think we see you
In the curtains looking in between
Just open the door
And say Happy Halloween

HATERS

There are so many things
That are the same
From day to day
In life's game
People wishing and dreaming
On the stars above
To show them
That one true love
Maybe to find
That pot of gold
Or that précis gem
For them to hold
But there is one thing
We can do without
It is the one thing we
Can do something about
I'm sure you know
The very thing
It's the hate
That haters bring

Hi I think you know me

Hi I think you know me
I'm not sure but I think you do
Or maybe it's that you forgot me
But I'm someone you knew
I haven't been around lately
I admit I should have kept in touch
I know you are really busy
But my life has became a bit much
I know that you have a plan for all
And sometimes you give us a test
That if I really believe
I would let my worries rest
There are times when I look in the mirror
I don't recognize my own face
I was wondering if it's no trouble
If you would take me from this place
I know that everyone has their own time
And that you will know
I don't think I'm that important here
No one will truly miss me I really want to go
If not then show me what I must do
I really want to leave
I'll do whatever you say
Forever yours one who believes

Highway of lies

I saw you the other day
Walking with someone new
I could not believe my eyes
No this can't be true
You kissed him so tenderly
I thought my heart would break
I had to close my eyes
This has to be a mistake
You come home
I look into your eyes
Now I can really see
Your highway of lies
You tell me you love me
I thought I would die
I tell you I love you too
I just want to break down and cry
You said your love was true
Now I can really see
You must think I'm some kind of fool
The way you are using me
You hold me in your arms
I look into your eyes
Now I can really see
Your highway of lies

HOME IS WHERE YOU ARE

I cuddle up close
In your arms
Trying to show you
My loving charm
You turn and look
With a smile so bright
That it turns
Darkness to light
In your arms
Is where I'll be
Knowing that
The whole world can see
What can I say
I'm in love
I'll shout it from down below
And up above
From you
I'll never go far
Cause my love
Home is where you are

I AM ALONE

I walk around this crowded room
As people smile and wave
They stop and say hello
A simple hi from my lips is all I crave
People joke people laugh
People talk people sing
That's when I know
I am alone
I walk down the street
They smile as they pass
The faces I should know
I dismiss them with a tip of a hat
People walk people talk
People dream people scream
That's when I know
I am alone
I feel the warmth from your skin
As I lay here next to you
Looking into your eyes
I see the deepest blue
You say you love me
With a tear I say I love you too
That's when I know
I am alone

I NEED TO KNOW

I stand here all alone
And I don't know why
You said you would
Always be by my side
And now
You had to go
What can I do
I need to know
You left me here
And I hate you
Now I really know
Your words where not true
And still
You had to go
What can I say
I need to know
They all say you didn't mean to
And I know that's true
I didn't mean what I said
I really love you
I guess I'll say goodbye
You had to go
Why did you have to die
I need to know

I PROMISE YOU

Would you like to
Have all the gold
All for you
Just to hold
How would you like
Some precise gems
Diamonds maybe rubies
I would recommend
How about a
Great big ship
Or a giant pool
For a dip
Now here's the deal
And I'll make it clear
All you have to do
Is just sign here
Yeah that's it
Now here's the plan
And I know that
You will understand
Now here's the price
And you'll think I'm bold
All it will cost
Is your soul
Remember, I'm going to make all
Your dreams come true
All this and more
I promise you

I WON'T TELL

Come here daddy's girl
Let's play a game
Daddies going to touch you there
And you won't be the same
Hush now princess
Don't make daddy yell
I promise you daddy
I won't tell
Come here boy
Do as your told
I'll beat you again
You're not too old
Now see what you've done
You made me yell
I promise you daddy
I won't tell
I have to tell you
I want you to know
This happens everyday
Anyplace you go
I'm going to make you listen
Even if I have to yell
This will never stop
If no one tells

IF I WAS BLIND

If I was blind
I would not have to see
All the impurities
That make up me
Like this funny nose
Or that I'm fat
Or maybe I'm ugly
Imagine that
Then I would miss
All the wonderful things
Like the new flowers
That comes in the spring
Like the soaring eagles
That fly in the sky
Or the little brooks
That flow gentle by
Like the wonderful art
That is made by mankind
I would miss all of these
If I was blind

IF ONLY IN MY MIND

I see the bright light
So beautiful to behold
I see heaven's gates
All made of gold
I hear the angels sing
He also loves my kind
I feel the warmth of his touch
If only in my mind
In the line of duty
All the blood I've spilled
They're last breathe escapes
They're eyes go still
My salvation is still there
I see the sign
He whispers his love
If only in my mind
There's no escape
From what I've done
Cheered by all
Loved by none
A hero's welcome
Is what I'll find
Redemption is there
If only in my mind

IF ONLY YOU

My love for you only grows
Each day as the day goes
My heart is filled by you
If only you knew
I sit by the riverside
Watching it flow gently by
Wishing you were here by me
If only you could see
I scream and curse your name
Wishing it could be the same
Screaming I want you near
If only you could hear
Looking over the graves
Hoping they are all saved
Reading what should be read
If only you were not dead

IF YOU

If you want to know
What's on my mind
It's the way I feel for you
In every way and kind
If you want to hear
What it has to say
Just put your ear to my heart
It will always speak that way
If you want to see
What's in my heart
Just lift your head
Look into my eyes
If you want to feel
What I have for you
Let me hold you in my arms
Take in all my love that's true

If you had a wish

If I had just one wish
That I knew would come true
I know what it would be
And that would be you
To be in your arms
Held so tight
Kisses your lips
Till the morning light
Just to be with you
To walk hand and hand
To lay on the beach
Or to walk in the sand
To dance with you
Under the stars
One look in your eyes
Would take me so far
To make love to you
That's what it would be
But if you had a wish
What would it be

IF YOU MUST KNOW

If you must know
What is the deal
Well sit right down
And I'll tell you right here
You say I look angry
You say I look pissed
Just sit right there
And I'll tell you this
I'm just plain evil
Right down to the core
If you don't believe me
I'll tell you some more
I can torture and kill
And I wouldn't think twice
I can even tell you
That I would think it was nice
Now don't tell me I need love
That's not what I'm trying to resist
How can anyone love
Something as mean as this

IMAGINE A WORLD

Imagine a world
Where people are free
To be anything
They wanted to be
To say anything
They wanted to say
To pray the way
They wanted to pray
To be together
Without being torn apart
To love the one
That they hold in their hearts
Not to be judged
By the color of they're skin
But to be seen for
The beauty within
Where hatred cannot be seen
Not even a trace
And love is the only
Feeling in this place
Now close your eyes
And take it all in
Imagine this world
Now let it begin

In my heart

There is someone I love
He is my everything
Without him
I would have nothing
He makes the darkest day
Shine so bright
When I fall into darkness
He is my light
He makes me happy
When I am sad
He makes me calm
When I am mad
He soothes me
When I am scared
He protects me
He is always there
Where is he
Why are we apart
We're not he's up above
And in my heart

IN MY MIND

They come to me at night
Whispering my name
Night after night
It's all the same
Safe place from these voices
I cannot find
Or is it all
In my mind
They come to me at night
Not showing their faces
Promising to show me
All kinds of places
Under the covers I go
I wish I were blind
Or is it all
In my mind
They come to me at night
All those demons
All growling at me
To join they're legion
I wish I were strong
But I was never that kind
Or is it all
In my mind

IN THE DARK OF THE NIGHT

Darkness is coming
You feel something's wrong
You don't know what it is
But you know you're strong
That feeling is still there
But you're sure you'll be alright
I'm coming for you
In the dark of the night
The feeling is stronger
As darkness falls
You see the shadows
On the walls
You start to fear
In the fading light
I'm coming for you
In the dark of the night
You smell my stench
You hear me all around
You try to run
You fall to the ground
You start to feel
You'll die of fright
I am here for you
In the dark of the night

IN THE SHADOWS

I'm kept safe
Where no one knows
My safe place
Will never show
In the darkness
Is where I will be
Staring out hoping
No one will see me
In the shadows
My face
I must hide
My fears
I must keep inside
In the darkness
Is where I will be
Looking down hoping
No one will know me
In the shadows
My tears
They stain my face
My cries
They stay in this place
In the darkness
Is where I will be
Wondering why
No one will save me
In the shadows

INVISIBLE ME

I stand here in the dark
So you can't see me
I whisper to myself
So you can't hear me
I close my eyes
And wonder why
You try to hurt me
I laugh out loud
So you don't know it
That I'm crying inside
But I don't show it
I whisper up to him
But you don't know
How much I mean to him
If they take a look around
Will they see it
The question of the world
Will they answer it
If they look behind
Will they see
The monster that I see
If they closed they're eyes
Would they really see
That inside they look just like me

It Seems

It seems to me
There's only one day
Where everyone
Wants to behave
Where people seem
To really not mind
And all in all
People are kind
Where everyone smiles
And waves at each other
And everyone is treated
Like a sister or brother
Where all the fighting
Seems to cease
And just for one day
We all have world peace
Why is it that it's
Just for one day
That everyone seems
To reflect on their ways
Were the skies parted
And the angels sent
To show us all
Joy and merriment
What is this feeling
We cannot hold on to
From day to day
The whole year through
We should have these feeling
Of hope and dreams
Not just on Christmas
But through the year, it seems

JUST A DREAM

I hold your hand
People stare as they walk by
I look into your eyes
They're as blue as the sky
I kiss your lips
As I hold you tight
My fingers run through your hair
It shines in the light
We walk to the park
Down by the brook
I was in love with you from the start
One glance was all it took
Our love will shine for all times
Or so it seams
I look up and see you with him
And know it was just a dream

JUST FOR YOU

What is this feeling
I feel inside
It starts in my heart
Then it multiplies
What is this feeling
It's something new
It started when
I first saw you
I felt this feeling
When I saw you there
With the rays of the sun
Shining in your hair
I know this feeling
And it is true
It's the love that I have
Just for you

LAND OF MY FATHERS

In the land of my fathers
Where the deer roam
That is where
I call my home
The white man came
And took it away
Now nothing will
Be the same
In the land of my fathers
Where the beaver dam
And the great waters
Surround the land
The eagles soar
Up in the sky
The land of my fathers
Is where I will die

LIFE OR DEATH

Life it hurts
No matter where we go
Death would free us
This we know
Why do we cling
To this life of pain
Tears we cry
Our faces stain
Life or death
What do we choose
Darkness is coming
There's no time to lose
Death is calling
So why do we wait
We are so close
To Heaven or Hell's gates
Let's make the cut
We're getting cold
The angel of death is here
With a kiss he takes our soul

KNEEL AT MY FEET

I walk into the room
I feel the power
Night is coming
It is my hour
You start to shake
As you stand
You bend over
And kiss my hand
You look up
Waiting for your treat
I look down at you
Kneel at my feet
On your knees
You make a bow
Happy there is
No pain for now
I walk to my thrown
And I sit down
I look to the place
You should be found
You scramble to me
Waiting to be beat
I yell down to you
Kneel at my feet
I grab the whip
And place it on your back
You tense up
Waiting for the attack
I hesitate and that's
All it took
You stand up
To take a look
In a moment
Our eyes meet
Then you scream
Kneel at my feet

LIGHTHOUSE

The lighthouse is that special light
At the harbor shining so bright
To bring the ships safely in
Whenever a storm begins
You are a lighthouse too
To everyone that is blue
Wrapping them in a warm embrace
Till all their sadness is erased
Animals are not ignored
Helping all that come to your door
This is just your way
And no one is turned away
The world is a better place
Just to see that smile on your face
We are blessed and that is true
And we all thank you

This poem was written
In memory for Deanna Prout

LOOK FOR HIM

When you're stumbling
And don't know what to do
You hear people talking
And you don't know what is true
He is there
Listen to him
When you are lost
And it feels like its everyday
You sit there alone
Cause you don't know what to say
He is there
Talk to him
When you are in the dark
And there is nothing in sight
You are wondering around
Looking for the light
He is by your side
Look for him

LOOK INSIDE

Life is not easy
No matter what they say
Like the image in the mirror
That just won't go away
You say you're ugly
You say you're fat
You say you're stupid
And nothing will change that
You just want to disappear
You just want that hiding place
No matter what kind
Maybe it's with drugs
That you know you can find
Maybe it's in the bottle
Drink till you go blind
Maybe with a knife
You know what they say
With just a slice
All the pain goes away
Maybe you just need
To know that you are loved
Just look inside
Then to heaven above

Lost

I ask around
Hoping to find
That person inside
No matter what kind
My search is deep
It's taken its toll
It's driving me mad
It's taking my soul
It's taken me over
I'm on the ground
I try to scream
I can't make a sound
I'll try to fight
No matter the cost
I already know
My soul is lost

Meet me

I say we are the same
Me and you
In everything we say
In everything we do
Together forever
That's what we'll be
Darkness is coming
Meet me
It's getting time now
Grab that knife
Let's go out
And take a life
No time to hesitate
There's blood to see
Darkness is coming
Meet me
You coward
Where's your spine
They did us wrong
I want what's mine
You will do as you're told
There's nowhere to flee
Darkness is coming
Meet me
What's the matter
Yeah it's true
Look in that mirror
I am you
There is no one here
To hear your plea
Darkness is coming
Meet me

Memory

The memory of you
Still rings in my head
I sit hear alone
Now that you're dead
With my head hung low
And tears in my eyes
I just can't make
The days go by
In my heart
You will always stay
Throughout the years
Day after day after day

MIRACLES

People pray for miracles
Not knowing what kind
They're praying and hoping
It's just a matter of time
Miracles they happen
Every minute of the day
The minute they happen
People don't know what to say
Like the birth of a child
Oh what a joy
Just watching it grow
Whether a girl or a boy
The death of winter's grip
When snow covers the plains
With the kiss of springs sun
Life begins again
Life is a miracle
That we all know
And the meaning of life
Is the whole show
The greatest miracle
I know it's a must
Is the power of love
And what it brings us
So when you find love
I want you to know
No matter who or what's said
Never let it go

My awakening

As the village
Starts their day
With hast
They make their way
Rushing out the door
Into the street
Waving their hand
At all they meet
Before long
They will be out of time
As someone cries
How could we be so blind
For they all see
The sun is falling
And they all know
Who that will be calling
Now they all rush home
And into bed
Praying by morning
They are not all dead
For now
All the church bells ring
To sound
My awakening

My black heart

There is one thing
I want you to know
I will help you
Anywhere you go
I will give you
Everything you need
I will love you
You don't have to plea
You are the only one
That I will see
The other means nothing
You can trust me
All you wish for
Right from the start
You can trust me
Cross my black heart

MY HALO

My halo shines so bright
To help me see through the night
I'm a good little boy
With all my toys
I'm an angel in flight
That's right
There are times I may be bad
Mischievous at times but glad
I get into trouble
But I swear it's my double
I swear with all my might
That's right
My halo shines so bright
And you say that something's not right
You say you are torn
Cause they are made out of horns
But aren't they a hell of a sight
That's right

MY LOVE

From heaven above
Nor hell below
I never knew
Which way to go
Then you walked in
And took my heart
And told me
We would never part
I love each time
You draw me near
Now that my heart
Knows no fear
As I look into
Your eyes so blue
I see things
I never knew
I'll gladly walk
Away from the darkness
As you fill my heart
With such happiness
I miss you every time
You're gone from my side
And filled with joy
When I see you with my eyes
My love what I'm
Trying to say
I love you more
With each day

This poem was written for
Yrkra Yifu a good friend

My misery

I have a date with destiny
And no one will know
Oh look at the time
I really have to go
One last look
To check my face
I will escape
Without a trace
I really shouldn't
Be surprised
My misery
I will realize
Like they planed
I'm by the jail
They sent me his face
And all his details
I take my shot
His shirt stained red
With one bullet
He falls dead
They start to shoot
With their guns
My misery
Has begun
I round the corner
As bullets fly past
Adrenalin is pumping
My heart is beating fast
I rip off the face
To reveal my own
A bullet flies
My skin is torn
I run to the docks
And make the gate
My misery
Will be my fate

My Mother

There is a woman
That my love is true
From the very day
That I was new
At night
She tucked me in
She was there
Through thick and thin
When I was hurt
She was there for me
Now I'm older
She set me free
Looking back
I never knew
All the things
I put her through
She is my teacher
And my best friend
And I will love her
Till the end
I am a good man
She taught me well
In her eyes I hope
I never fail
Knowing her
I'm truly blessed
Now that I'm older
She can get some rest
In my eyes
There will be no other
Who is she
She is my Mother

This poem is for my Mother
I Love You So Much

MY PRISON OF PAIN

I'm locked in this cage
Inside my mind
Till they decide
How to dispose of my kind
What was my crime
That put me in here
Maybe it was causing
So many tears
My clothes are red
My soul is stained
Maybe I belong in
My prison of pain
They told me
About my animal past
I don't believe I cried
I don't remember that
But what they say
Must be true
My anger
Is nothing new
My clothes are red
My soul is stained
Maybe I belong in
My prison of pain
I hang my head
And start to weep
There is silence
Not even a peep
No more voices
Do I hear
No more rage
No more tears
My clothes are red
My soul is stained
I fear I will die in
My prison of pain

My Sins Are Many

The shadow is my home
And it's been since I was born
I hide my face
From every place
My sins are many I'm told
The shadow keeps me safe
And I know I'm in the right place
The voices soar
With a mighty roar
My sins are many I'm told
The shadow is where I must hide
From all the tears that I cried
Like blood from a dove
I know I can't love
My sins are many I'm told
The shadow is where I have been
To hide the color of my skin
Why can't they see
We are all human beings
My sins are many I'm told

NEVER

I look in your eyes
And see the passion
You lean in as you
Whisper your questions
Telling me all those things
Other people say
Telling you that
I will not stay
Telling you that
Someone has taken your place
As I watch the tears
Running down your face
I reach out
With a gentle touch
Telling you that
I love you so much
Telling you not to
Listen to them not ever
From you side I will not leave
Never

No one can know

I stand here looking around
Crying on the inside
Hoping no one can see
How much I want to die
I don't care
Where I will go
I know in my heart
No one can know
The pain is deep
In my heart
My soul feels like
It's being torn apart
I fear that
It is starting to show
I have to hide
No one can know
I cannot stand
The pain in my head
It's driving me mad
I wish I were dead
I have to stop this
This I do know
But if I do
No one can know

Nowhere to go

You see me there
Out on the street
You look away
So our eyes don't meet
For my sins are many
And my soul is stained
For causing so many
So much pain
You judge, sentence
And torture me
For the crime
Of being me
For this you say
My soul must bleed
For all my
Unknowing deeds
From up above
To down below
I have
Nowhere to go

OCEAN OF TEARS

You use to be here with me
Now you're with someone new
You said you would love me forever
You said your love was true
How could you just
Turn your back and walk away
How can you say you love me
Then deny what you say
Now you're gone
And I'm still here
Now here comes
The ocean of tears
I thought I would die
When you said goodbye
Now all I can do
Is sit here and cry
What did I do
To turn you away
What can be said
To make you stay
Now you're gone
And I'm still here
Now here comes
The ocean of tears
Now get your things
And get them packed
Get out the door
And don't look back
I hope you can pay
What it will cost
Cause you'll never know
What you lost
Now you're gone
And I'm still here
Now here comes
The ocean of tears

One heartbeat left

I'm on the hunt
You are my prey
Nothing you can do
Nothing you can say
Run and hide
Yeah do your best
You don't know
You have one heartbeat left
Turn around
I'm behind you
I see your fear
If you just knew
Yes try and fight
Yeah do your best
You don't know
You have one heartbeat left
I take my knife
It makes a thud
I see your pain
I feel your blood
I look into your eyes
I want to stress
I see your soul
You have one heartbeat left

ONE ROSE FOR YOU

Knocking at your door at sixteen
Trying to stand on shaking knees
Not really ready for the beauty
That was there before me
My heart was pounding
It was all so new
I looked into your eyes and smiled
One rose for you
Ten years later
Our lives was to begin
I kissed your lips
As I pulled you in
I got down on one knee
To show my love was true
With a ring tied to it
One rose for you
Now just six years later
You're gone away
As I stand here alone
I don't know what to say
I loved you so much
I hope you knew
As I brush the leaves away from your stone
One rose for you

ONE TRUE RACE

I hear people talking
About the one true race
And that everyone
Should know their place
So I thought for a moment
And found it was true
We need to start to believe
Starting with me and ending with you
This is so big
I will shout from sea to sea
And I think it is good news
I hope you agree
So now I'll tell you
Who is the one true race
It's not black or white
It's called the human race

Open mind

Would you like
To see a unicorn
Or maybe some
Chocolate popcorn
Or maybe you want
Hate to go
And to see
Love grow
Maybe you want
Purple trees
And with that
To have world peace
Maybe you want
The colors to fall
And to see people
For who they are
Are you looking
For people who are kind
Yes you can have all these
With an open mind

Outside looking in

The party is starting
The guest are all here
The guest of honor
Is standing over there
Friends and family
Is all that I see
They are all joking and laughing
Is it because of me
I want to know
What was my sin
That put me here
On the outside looking in
I know I shouldn't
Feel this way
I want to run
But I know I should stay
Why do I feel
So empty inside
I'm not able
To just get by
I know it now
This will be the end
No longer will I be
On the outside looking in

People like me

I sit down and look around
At the people around me
Little and tall, big and small
Do they know about me
The thoughts that grow in my mind
Are they thinking about me
The colors fade to a pale grey
Or is it just me
The hate I see in their eyes
Is it for me
I shake my head and wonder
Can they really see me
I just want to scream
You're people like me

PHOTOGRAPH OF YOU

I walk around
From room to room
Looking at everything
That reminds me of you
Running my fingers
Over everything I see
Knowing how lucky
That you were with me
With tears in my eyes
A cool breeze on my chin
Trying to remember
Everyplace we have been
I loved you so much
And I hope you knew
I'm just standing here looking
At a photograph of you
I don't want you to worry
I'm going to be alright
I'm going to wait right here
Till I have you back in my sight
There were so many places
We wanted to see
But we had fun
You and me
I loved you so much
And I hope you knew
I'm just standing here looking
At a photograph of you
I have to be strong
Once I had it all
Just one more look
Then I'll walk through the wall

Please tell me

I come to you
With a plea
I want to know if you
Will stay with me
I know I cheated
And I have no right
I have changed
I have seen the light
It is only you I love
I see that now
And it is your will
That I will bow
So hear my cries
Hear my plea
Will you stay
Please tell me

QUEEN OF DARKNESS

You sit on your thrown
And I'm at your feet
You look down at me
And our eyes meet
I put my head down
I look to the ground
I do not move
I don't make a sound
I feel the heat
Of your touch
I want more
I want it too much
I feel your nails
I feel the pain
It drives me wild
It drives me insane
My will is yours
My soul is too
Away from your side
Will never do
I will always walk
The forever darkness
Because you are my
Queen of darkness

Rain

What is rain
That falls from up high
Is it really water
From the clouds in the sky
Or is it the moisture
In the air
And it falls
Here and there
Or is it God
With a watering hose
Spraying the earth
For things to grow
No it's none of these
And it's time you knew
It's tears from the angels
Crying for you

RIVER OF BLOOD

I'm taken a boat
Down to hell
I have all these
Souls to sell
The path was born
From the flood
Of the souls I took
On the river of blood
The sail of flesh
The mast of bone
I as the captain
With my heart of stone
As I pull my anchor
Out of the mud
I plot my course
On the river of blood
I always have
Room for you
What you did
It's nothing new
I swing my sickle
With a mighty thud
Another soul is claimed
On the river of blood

SAVE THE CHILDREN

Come sit on my knee child
And tell me what you want
I want my mom and dad back
Come sit on my knee child
And tell me where they went
The lord took them away
Two years ago today
There is nothing I can do
If your mom and dad are dead
She slid off my knee
Turned, smiled, then slowly faded away
I learned something
That day in December
Save the children
From all harm
Save the children
From all illness big or small
Save the children
Or cherish a memory

SAY GOODBYE

Standing here with you
Looking out at the sea
Remembering how great it was
When you was here with me
Kissing and hugging you
Thinking of the time we have in store
Now holding this box
Wishing I had more
Standing here now
Just getting mad
Hating myself for
The thoughts I had
Now I throw this box
Into the sea
Where I know
You wanted to be
Hoping and praying
You're somewhere above
Knowing just how much
You were truly loved
With tears running down my face
I look up to the sky
Trying to find the words
To say goodbye

SHOEMAKER

Little shoemaker
Please make me a shoe
It has to fit right
And it has to be new
Little shoemaker
Please make it for me
I'll pay for it now
For my sweet Tiffanie

This poem was written
For my Daughter Tiffanie

Show me

You say that there's
Nothing that you fear
You say no one
Has seen your tears
You say that there is no one
You would flee
Talk is cheap
Show me
You say that no one
Can make you look down
You say that no one
Can make you look like a clown
You say that no one
Will hear you plea
Talk is cheap
Show me
You say all this
But it's all talk
I see all of these
Let's go for a walk
Tell me this
Who are you trying to be
Talk is cheap
Show me

SOMEONE SAVE ME

I grab a knife
I make a slice
I fall to my knees
As I start to bleed
I start to plea
Someone save me
I look around
As I lay on the ground
I fall apart
I want to stab my heart
I start to plea
Someone save me
I look above
And see a dove
My blood still flows
As I start to go
I start to plea
Someone save me
I see a light
It shines so bright
I feel the touch
I needed so much
I look up to see
The one who's saving me

SONGS OF THE DAMNED

Hello there
Do I have news for you
I'm going to put an end
To everything you knew
Yes I am afraid
It's you're time
And now you will have to pay
For all those beautiful crimes
Yes indeed
You've been a bad, bad boy
But I have to tell you
I love all you're bad, bad toys
Oh, you won't need your coat
You'll be plenty warm
No need for an umbrella
It never storms
Go ahead look around
No one to cry for you
Go ahead and plea
That's what they all try to do
All that blood money
That you spent
To silence all who saw
Was it worth every cent
Well it bought the best spot
On the lake of fire
To hear your torment
Is my desire
With that said I think
We'll get along just fine
Do you like music
Well you will have one hell of a time
The demons scream and hellhounds howl
And here I am
Now I give you
Songs of the damned

MY STAIRWAY OF BONES

I go out each night
And take a life
Their blood each stain
The blade of my knife
I like to smile
As I look back
My heart is dark
My soul is black
I'm making a path to Hell
With my heart of stone
Soon I will descend
My stairway of bones
Soon I'll take my place
By his side
You will not miss me
You will not cry
I will serve him
You will too
My pain will be legend
His bidding I will do
I'm making my path to Hell
With my heart of stone
Soon I will descend
My stairway of bones

STARDREAM

Close your eyes
It's time to sleep
I don't want to hear a word
Not even a peep
Drift off to the place
Of hope and dreams
Of candy canes
And stars that gleam
You're going there
So it seems
To the land of wishes
And stardreams
Where what you wish for
All come true
Where everything is there
Just for you
Now go there
Have the time of your life
Go have fun
You'll see I'm right
You're there now
Where the stars gleam
Now go have yourself
A stardream

This poem was writing
For my good friend Dannynice Kid
And his club

Stubs

I have a boy
I truly love
That no one
Can rise above
I take him
Wherever I go
He is mine
And everyone knows
No one in this world
Can take his place
He makes me smile
When I look at his face
In my heart
He is loved
No one is like
My dog stubs

TAKE ME THERE

You say there is a world
Filled with wonderful things
Yes, like people who are treated the same
There is no hatred or anything
The waters blue, the grass is green
And no pollution in the air
No bombs, guns, or war to think of
Not anything to beware
Where the birds sing with the choir
The trees and the people dance to their tune
Where things are really not that bad
And the only news is good news
Where you love the one in your heart
Right from the very start
No one says or tries anything
To rip you apart
I'm hooked tell me more
Like are there flowers in the spring
Oh my yes like I said
It is filled with wonderful things
Like the town has a meal
Cooked with care once a year
And the whole town
Is full of cheer
You tell me all of this
And it's not fair
You've been to this world
Now take me there

TEARS

Tears they have
There own little reasons
Like the world has its
Change of seasons
Tears can be from when
You're happy, sad, glad or mad
And none of these
Are really bad
Happy tears at
A child's birth
Sad tears when a
Love one leaves this earth
Glad tears when
You graduate
Mad tears when
You miss a date
For this is the ying and yang
On life ends another begins
Now you're ready to begin your life
And maybe you're not for them
For all of these
Make us grow
And there is one more thing
You need to know
All these and more
Are in life's plans
And all of that is
In God's hands

TEARS OF BLOOD

Come my darling
It is time
For you to walk
That endless line
I'm glad we
Can finely meet
Now you are
Mine to keep
No need to cry
That I can think of
Come now let's wipe away
Those tears of blood
I have waited for you
For a long long time
Now my dear
You will be mine
To me now
You will always be true
My love my dear
Will only be for you
No need to cry
That I can think of
Come now let's wipe away
Those tears of blood

THE DARKNESS

I want the darkness
To swallow me
To take me whole
So I can be
In its arms
Held so tight
So I can't see
Any light
I want the darkness
To hold me there
So I can't move
So I won't dare
So I can't breath
Or make a sound
So I can't even
Touch the ground
I want the darkness
To punish me
To make my soul
Start to bleed
Make this I swear
My dying wish
I'll go to hell
Just for this

THE GREAT TURTLE

The great turtle
Rose at night
Stretching its legs
With all its might
Stretching its neck
For it to see
But all it saw
Were only trees
The white man came
And built a fort
Their only way
Was war of some sort
The turtle saw this
And put its head down
Never again
Would it look around
The white man don't know
But my people do
The great turtle came up at night
And will go down that way too

The magic of death

Bury my soul deep in a bed
In the rotting flesh of a thousand men
Bury my body deep in the ground
So my bones cannot make a sound
Watch as the darkness takes over me
Let the world watch so they can see
Worship the knife that is stained
With the blood of my pain
Dance in the pool of my blood
Take the knife and start the flood
Wash away the ones who are not blessed
This is the magic of death

THE MESSENGER

War is coming
Choose your side
Light or dark
There's nowhere to hide
Who do you fight for
Why must it be
You fight for your souls
So you can be free
Look there he is
With songs like the dove
Who shines his bright light
From heaven above
But darkness is coming
So do not wait
He'll take you with him
Down to hell's gate
Now choose your side
There's no time to lose
Your soul is the only
Thing that will do
Don't get angry
I don't know what's in store
For I'm just the messenger
And nothing more

THE MONSTER INSIDE ME

I hide in the dark
So you don't know
The thing inside me
That only grows
It rips and tares
Trying to get free
I can't let out
The monster inside me
It's getting hard
If you just knew
You're in danger
It's after you
It's getting out
I start to plea
I can't hold back
The monster inside me
My tears they fall
As it grabs a knife
It's getting dark
Run for your life
It makes its stab
It finds its mark
It goes right through
My beating heart
I know it now
It had to be
I had to kill
The monster inside me

THERE IS A WORD

There is a word
With all its might
That will make you smile
All through the night
There is a word
Without any fear
That will make you happy
With every tear
There is a word
With a mighty roar
That will make your heart
Forever soar
There is a word
That's pure as a dove
That shows how I feel
That word is love

This poem was written
For my sister Shari
And her new Husband Leonard

UNDERSTAND

You stumble and cry
There's nowhere to go
Tears stain your face
You think no one knows
That you feel like
You're on a runaway train
That no one really
Knows your pain
You feel like your soul
Is being torn apart
But you have to hide
You can't show that part
If they saw that
What would they say
They would probably turn
And run away
I want to help you
Let's give it a try
Come to me my child
Please do not cry
I know your worries
I feel your pain
So let's try and stop
That runaway train
Now show me that neck
And be still as can be
It's time for me to drink
So you can be free
Understand this
And all will be well
Understand this is
Going to hurt like hell

VOICES

Voices are screaming
In my head
They torture me
With what they've said
They tell me that
You are gone
And with them
I now belong
They say love is
Waiting for me
And beautiful things
For me to see
With you I
Want to stay
They're begging me
To turn away
Come to me
I can't see you
There's this feeling
It's something new
What is this warmth
It is soothing me
They are telling me
To turn and see
I close my eyes
It shines so bright
They are telling me
To walk to the light
The voices are silent
I am in the light
I am with him now
And darling I'll be all right

WALK WITH ME

My tears they flow
With what is said
The hatred is still
Ringing inside my head
Why is there hatred
Why must there be
He whispers
Sit with me
People are talking
Isn't that great
I wish they would go
And take they're bigotry and hate
Why don't they just leave
And let me be
He whispers
Talk to me
I stumble around
Not knowing where to go
Why is there hatred
I just want to know
We are all the same on the inside
Why don't they see
He whispers
Walk with me

WALKIN' IN YESTERLAND

I saw her once
Walkin' after midnight
I knew a man who
Walked the line
I knew a man who
Wore a nudie suit
Singing those lonesome blues
In his cowboy boots
I know you'll think I'm crazy
But I got myself a plan
I'm going to keep on walkin'
Walkin' in yesterland
I knew a man who
Was crazy in love with make believe
And a man with a room full of roses
You never wanted to leave
There was a man who
Was king of rock and roll
And when he swiveled his hips
He always stole the show
I know you'll say I'm crazy
But I know it be would so grand
To be out there walkin'
Walkin' in yesterland
There were so many great people
Who helped us up or got us by
Like the president with his words of hope
Whose son saluted his final goodbye
There were so many great people
Who got up to fight for what was right
And I want to thank them all now
Especially the ones who paid the final price
I know it might sound crazy
But I can't wait to join the band
Lord I can see them now
Walkin' in yesterland

WALKING BETWEEN THE SHADOWS

Time in a bottle
Or footprints in the sand
No one really knows
Where I really stand
I know you're looking
But can you really see
What it is like
To really be me
Where am I going
I don't really know
I'm just happy
Walking between the shadows
When you look
You really don't see
What you're looking at
Is not really me
You say I'm not normal
That I don't belong
Tell me what is normal
What did I do wrong
Where am I going
I don't really know
I'm just happy
Walking between the shadows
Mama told me
You'll be a strong man
So go ahead and look
Cause I don't give a damn
If you just look
With tainted eyes
Then you really are
Just fucking blind
Where am I going
I really don't know
But I must keep on
Walking between the shadows

WE BECOME ONE

I saw you there
My heart fluttered
You touched my hand
I melted like butter
Our first date
How did I get that far
Our first kiss
I saw stars
The first time
I met your dad
I made it through
Boy was I glad
When I gave you a ring
You shined like the sun
Now on our wedding day
We become one

This poem was written
For my nephew Josh
And his new wife Nicole

Welcome to my Mind

Don't mind those bones
I didn't have time to clean
There is a path right there
Just walk between
Everything you are looking for
I hope you will find
I hope you have fun
Welcome to my mind
Don't be silly
I don't mind the mud
As you see
I still have all this blood
Yes I like you
You are one of a kind
I'm sorry if I stare
Welcome to my mind
Don't be scared now
You will have fun
We just have to wait
Till the setting sun
I'm afraid you have to stay here
You will have one hell of a time
You wanted to look
Welcome to my mind

WHERE THE EAGLE SOARS

I want to walk with the great father
Up where the great spirits are
Where I can be free
To walk among the stars
I want to stand with the great father
To watch over my people too
To watch him guide them
In everything they do
I want to sit with the great father
To hear the great bears mighty roar
As I look down at my people
From where the eagle soars

Who are we

We are superior
To everything
No matter what some say
Or the words they bring
We are the kings
Of everything we see
So tell me this
Who are we
Some will say that we are ignorant
In what we think of ourselves
That we should come down from our high horse
And put that thought back on the shelves
We are the only ones
How else can it be
But tell me this
Who are we
I want to know
What sets us apart
Who is the judge
Of who is smart
Why must we shoot first
Before we can see
Someone tell me this
Who are we

WHO ARE YOU

You say I should
Watch what I say
You say I should
Watch who I play
You say I should
Always say what's true
All I have to say is
Who are you

You say I should
Live by the book
You say I should
Give back what I took
You say I should
Start life anew
All I have to say is
Who are you

You say I should
Treat people right
You say I should
Look for the light
You say that I shouldn't
Make people blue
All I have to say is
Who are you

WHO IS GOD

Who is this God
That everyone prays to
That takes us to that place
When we have paid our dues
What is his name
We spilled all that blood
So many names
To think of
Who has the right God
For whom we should pray to
Should we tear them all down
And start anew
I'll tell you something
You all want to hear
There is only one God
No need for tears
For this one God
He has so many names
So many faces
But he is one in the same
He answers all
No matter how you pray
No matter where you are from
No matter what's your faith
To him we are one
And he is so proud
How do I know this
I know this God

WHY CAN'T YOU SEE

The words you say
Cut like a knife
The look you gave
Brings me to my knees
I just want to scream
Why can't you see
I hide in the dark
So you don't know
The words you say
Just won't go
I whisper to you please
Why can't you see
I lay here thinking in bed
Of the words you have said
Wondering why can't you see
That the person in the mirror
Staring at you is me

Will you save me

I look around
Not knowing where to go
I ask everyone
They all answer no
I wish I knew where I was
But I cannot see
All I ask is
Will you show me
I hear the whispers
I feel the stares
Something is telling me
To beware
I see it in the shadow
What can it be
All I ask is
Will you help me
It's getting dark
It starts to stand
I wish I could run
But I don't think I can
It starts to walk
I fall to my knees
All I pray is
Will you save me

WINGS

There are many wings
That fly above
From robins to blue jays
And bats and doves
The dragon's wings
I would like to see
Their mighty roar
Would bring me to my knees
From all the wings
That breaks the clouds crest
It's angels or is it demons
That I like the best
For its these two
I would have to say
That's in men's hearts
And that's where they'll stay

With the dead

I talk with the dead
I have no fear
They tell me things
I want to hear
I walk with the dead
They comfort me
They show me things
I want to see
I'll tell you something
You'll start to dread
I want to lie
With the dead

You don't see me

I touch you
Holding your hand
I brush your cheek
With the back of my hand
I reach out to you
But you don't feel me
I whisper your name
On the wings of a dove
Confessing to you
All of my love
I cry out to you
But you don't hear me
I stand here
Looking at your face
As your tears
Stain your face
I wave goodbye to you
But you don't see me